Minicalculators
IN THE CLASSROOM

The hand-held calculator, or minicalculator, has become an important piece of equipment in our everyday lives. Educators are discovering that it also has a significant place in the mathematics class, where it can help students perform the routine calculations that often deflect them from the more meaningful processes that must be mastered for a sound understanding of mathematics.

In this report in the *Developments in Classroom Instruction* series, Dr. Joseph R. Caravella, a member of the staff of the National Council of Teachers of Mathematics, explores the positive contributions of the minicalculator to basic education. He discusses the necessity for the equipment to be available for equal time periods to all students in a class so that it cannot become a means of locking out students with few economic advantages. He shows how the minicalculator can become a time-saver and an aid to conceptualizing in mathematics. He also describes its ability to bring the mathematics class closer to the everyday world through its use as a consumer tool. A group of classroom activities keyed to various functions of the minicalculator completes the report.

In her introduction to the report, Dr. E. Glenadine Gibb of the University of Texas at Austin, Past President of the National Council of Teachers of Mathematics, discusses the basic questions educators ask about the use of the minicalculator.

MINICALCULATORS

in the Classroom

Minicalculators
IN THE CLASSROOM

by Joseph R. Caravella

National Education Association
Washington, D.C.

Acknowledgments

The manuscript of this book was reviewed by Christopher J. Gregory, Elementary Supervisor, Silver Lake Regional School District, Massachusetts.

Library of Congress Cataloging in Publication Data

Caravella, Joseph R
    Minicalculators in the classroom.

    (Developments in classroom instruction)
    Bibliography: p.
    1. Calculating-machines. 2. Mathematics — Study
and teaching. I. Title. II. Series.
QA75.C37   510'.28   76-41213
ISBN 0-8106-1812-5 (paper)
        0-8106-1814-1 (cloth)

CONTENTS

Introduction

by E. Glenadine Gibb

Many teachers and school administrators find themselves faced with decisions concerning the use of calculators in the classroom as students bring them to school. Among the questions asked are:

- Should we permit use of calculators in the classroom?
- Can they be used effectively without compromising the development of mathematical understandings and competencies?
- What changes can be expected, if any, in the objectives of mathematics instruction and the school mathematics program if calculators are used in classrooms?
- What criteria should be used in buying calculators for school use?
- How can they be made available to all students in an equitable fashion?

Many schools are already making use of minicalculators in a variety of ways in the classroom. The National Council of Teachers of Mathematics supports the position that hand-held calculators can be effectively and creatively used as instructional aids in stimulating students' thinking. There is not, however, a unified position among teachers with respect to the benefits gained or the problems created by the use of minicalculators.

The research to date on the educational benefits of using them in the classroom is inconclusive, although there is some evidence that students who use them are more motivated and exhibit higher achievement than those who do not. Subjective observations, however, support use of these instruments in schools.

Let us consider the minicalculator as an instructional device.

For students in the lower elementary grades who have not developed a concept of numbers, a system for naming numbers, and an understanding of the meaning and processes of basic mathematical operations, the mechanics of pushing keys and reading what appears in the display on a calculator may only provide practice in numeral recognition skills. There is evidence, however, that the calculator can help the learning and thinking of students in the upper elementary and secondary schools.

Also, students in upper elementary schools and in junior and senior high schools enjoy using minicalculators. This, in turn, may stimulate their interest in learning in general and in learning mathematics in particular. This is especially true for those who have had unsuccessful experiences in mathematics.

Students can get excited, however, about novelty and machines. In such cases, one might then predict that when the novelty wears off, their interest will wane.

Teachers may ask students to use calculators in the following ways:

Checking answers. Students work a problem on paper and then with the calculator. If the calculator and its user disagree, who is correct? Is the machine or the operator malfunctioning? The analysis of "who is right" provides for more thoughtful analysis of a problem than checking responses in an answer book. In rechecking a computation, the calculator is also helpful in checking partial steps in the computation.

Debugging the problem. Students consider a multiplication problem such as $345 \times 283 =$ _____ . By finding 5×283, 40×283, and 300×283, they can check partial products. Or students can add long lists of figures by getting the sum of the whole list and by getting the sum of parts of the list and then adding those partial sums together. In a division computation, students can check products and subtractions. They can verify results by using the $\times$ key.

Checking knowledge of basic facts in addition, subtraction, multiplication, and division. Learners can engage in self-regulated exercises such as "racing" the calculator to see if they can name the answer before it appears on the display as they press the appropriate key. (Some teachers report that students who use minicalculators learn basic multiplication facts more quickly than their predecessors who used other devices.)

Assessing insight. After students complete a division computation, say, $322 \div 23$, they can solve the same problem on their calculators using the $-$ key. From 322 they can make continuous subtractions of 23 fourteen times. Without using the $\times$ key, students can find the product of 8×384 simply by adding 384 eight times.

Working with decimals. To use the calculator in working with fractions, it is often necessary to use the decimal representation of rational numbers instead of their usual fractional representation. By dividing the numerator by the denominator (i.e., by converting fractions to decimals), students can easily locate the rational numbers 3/4, 5/6, 2/3, and 7/8 on the number line.

Exploring number theory. After discussing ratios and the concept of identifying the basic fraction for a rational number, students can use their calculators, to identify common factors for numerators and denominators. Finding the prime factorization of a large number, such as 1,067,430, can deepen students' understanding of the number theory.

Making the calculator "speak." With an appropriate set of calculations, students can form words from the following eight letters: B, E, G, H, I, L, O, S. They may use the same letter more than once.

Then they may create calculations that result in a display where B = 8, E = 3, G = 6, H = 4, I = 1, L = 7, 0 = 0, S = 5. For example, to fail to win:

$(700 \times 5) + 7 =$ _____ .

To find the solution, students complete the computation and then turn the calculator upside down.

Making patterns. Students can generate number patterns with a calculator that they would not do otherwise because of the tedious computation. For example:

$1 \times 1 =$ _____

$11 \times 11 =$ _____

$111 \times 111 =$ _____

Now students guess:

$1111 \times 1111 =$ _____

$11111 \times 11111 =$ _____

$111111 \times 111111 =$ _____

Solving problems. Students can solve problems involving computations that would be tedious without the use of a minicalculator. For example, they can work the following:

• Find the unit price of various sized containers of a product and then compare the values.

• Determine how many seconds there are in a year.

• Using the measurements of at least 10 different circles, divide the circumference of each by its diameter and record the quotients. (In this manner, the value of pi is clearly illustrated to students.)

• Discover how many years it would take to double an investment at a rate of 7½ percent compounded annually, quarterly, and daily.

How may the use of calculators in the classroom change mathematics programs? With many calculators displaying solutions in decimal notation, we can expect the study of rational numbers, expressed as decimals, to appear earlier in the curriculum than has been customary. This change has already been anticipated with the projected shift to the metric system.

No doubt there will be a change in what and how we teach computation. Skills in estimating and error-checking will receive greater emphasis because minicalculators make it possible to receive immediate feedback of answers to complex calculations. At the same time, extensive use of minicalculators makes it more essential than before for students to know in what "ballpark" their answers should lie.

There will be greater emphasis on problem solving, especially problems from the real world for which finding solutions was previously prohibitive because of the need for tedious and laborious computation.

Many kinds of calculators are available. In making a decision to select suitable ones for classroom use, the purchaser should consider how they are to be used and the amount budgeted to buy them.

For beginners, buyers should buy calculators that have—

• An easy-to-read display with the same style numerals as those in textbooks

• A display of at least six or preferably eight digits

• Easily accessible spring-loaded click keys

• Four functions: $+$, $-$, $\times$, $\div$

• Floating decimal

• Two clearing keys (clear entry and clear)

- No key with dual purpose
- A notation of the operation hours of the battery and use of an AC adapter
- Algebraic logic.

As with other learning devices in the classroom, the calculators must be durable. The buyer should get them from a reliable company that gives a warranty on them and that can either repair them when they are damaged or can recommend another place where they can be repaired.

A few hundred dollars can buy a fair number of machines that can be shared by students and classes. It is not necessary that all students have a calculator at all times for the machines to be used effectively in the classroom. It is advisable, however, to have no more than two students using one at a time. Any higher ratio of students to calculator leads to student frustration, confusion, and dislike for the machine unless teachers develop teaming and sharing techniques.

In exploring the potential of calculators as a teaching device, teachers might start by using a dozen in class one or two days a week.

Like any other teaching aid, the calculator can create more problems than it can solve if it is misused. Although it will reduce the need for pencil-paper skills, it is not a substitute for them. Also, teachers cannot assume that just the introduction of a minicalculator in the classroom will necessarily motivate students.

Teachers should also guard against programming each move students make while using calculators. They should let them explore independently, for personal experience plays a great role in the learning process.

To place calculators in the hands of students just for the sake of using them can be disastrous. Students' mathematical capabilities can be enhanced, however, with the associated thinking and comprehension of the work that the calculators are doing for them. Creative use, after understandings have been abstracted, can establish the calculator as a valuable asset in today's mathematics classroom.

1. The Age of the Minicalculator

We have entered the age of the minicalculator. Indeed history may well consider the technical development of minicalculators in the United States as a bicentennial contribution to world progress.

Minicalculators have become an integral part of our society. Market analysts estimate that one out of every four Americans, including children, owns a calculator.[1] A basic model originally sold for $150. Today, the price of some models is less than $5, or about the same as other instructional aids. Hence these inexpensive, durable devices are available to most students.

→ Like desktop calculators and computers, the minicalculator was developed by industry without much concern for its impact on education. Some manufacturers, in cooperation with educators, have sorted through the maze of hardware and software and have developed specialized models for use in the classroom. However, many machines not suitable for schools will remain on the market for some time.

Although the minicalculator is useful for everyone, this report concentrates on the use of calculators within our educational system. The effective use of minicalculators in our schools may provide the mathematics educator with a challenge greater and more significant than that of "modern" mathematics or metrication.

Some Questions

Although many questions about minicalculators have been raised since they became available, educators are just beginning to gather data and probe the issues. Some of the questions that need to be answered are:

1. How and when will minicalculators influence curriculum and evaluation?
2. What effect will minicalculators have on classroom management?
3. Will the use of minicalculators interfere with the development of mathematical concepts and skills?
4. What do researchers say about the use of minicalculators in schools?
5. Can minicalculators of equal sophistication be made available to all students?
6. What financial considerations face school districts providing minicalculators for their students?
7. Are there types of minicalculators that are more appropriate for use by one age or ability group than another?
8. What guidelines are available for selecting a minicalculator?[2]

As classroom use of calculators increases, we can expect more questions, a variety of interpretations and a variety of conclusions. For the time being, we should look at some ways in which minicalculators are being used in the classroom.

Some Uses

The minicalculator is already making valuable contributions in the mathematics classroom. It is being used to save time, to reinforce learning, to develop concepts, to motivate the learner, and to apply mathematics in realistic, everyday situations. Minicalculators are quiet enough to be used in a library or study hall and versatile enough to be used wherever they can be carried.

Time Saver. The minicalculator obviously reduces computational time. Educators and students are reallocating their time and are becoming more efficient. Teachers can spend less time writing and correcting tests, and students less time taking tests. Teachers can use the time saved to design tests that evaluate the student's knowledge of mathematical concepts rather than of computational speed. Students may have more instructional time available as fewer classroom hours are spent on testing.

And they will get the kind of immediate feedback that reinforces learning by making the correction of tests possible in class because correction time is minimized by the use of minicalculators. Computational drudgery that wastes time, destroys interest, and inhibits learning may soon be a thing of the past.

Teachers can provide students with experiences that let them see what previously may have been discussed in theoretical terms only. Real-life problems are no longer too time-consuming to be considered for classroom discussion, since calculations too tedious for pencil-and-paper can now be accomplished with a calculator. The use of contrived problems, then, can be eliminated.

In today's compartmentalized society, we function in specialized blocks of time such as the school day, the work day, the science class, and the lunch hour. Within each block of time the resources vary. Since the minicalculator can virtually go wherever you go, there is a strong probability that it will be with you when you need it. Ideas can be tested and problems solved as they occur. Minicalculators are offering experiences and options that have been unavailable before.

Reinforcement. The minicalculator provides immediate reinforcement of definitions, functions, and basic properties. For example, calculators are convincing students that the product of two negative numbers is positive and that when you square the square root of a number you get the number. Machines with memories are helping students find limits and sum series.[3,4]

As a flexible answer key, the minicalculator provides immediate feedback for checking. It is replacing flash cards and other drill materials. A new way of evaluating one's knowledge of the basics is to match one's recall accuracy and speed against the time required to generate and display the same facts on a calculator.[5] In addition, tracing errors in complex computations is routine. Improved mathematical understanding and insight should follow.

Motivation. Minicalculators are generating interest in the mathematics classroom.[6,7,8,9] They can simplify computations and provide experiences that expand and reinforce concepts that previously were too impractical to consider. Students are becoming more inquisitive, creative, and independent as they experiment with minicalculators and mathematical ideas.[10] Generating and identifying unique number patterns and developing and playing calculator games are two popular types of student activities. There seems to be no end in sight to the number and variety of enrichment activities developing in the classroom since minicalculators appeared.

Conceptualization. Minicalculators are providing new opportunities to concentrate on understanding mathematical concepts. Number-systems concepts and an understanding of computational algorithms are being strengthened by the use of calculators.[11,12] Students are able to develop the analytical skills necessary to debug problems. In the classroom, understanding and thinking are emphasized rather than rote computations. Estimation and error-identification skills are being developed as a result of using minicalculators, whether the need for such skills is triggered by human error or by machine malfunction.[13,14]

Applications. The minicalculator brings the real world into the classroom. Problem solving is more realistic, since the numbers no longer have to be simple. Students are gathering, interpreting, and using data from experiences in their real world which includes all of the courses they take. With the help of the minicalculator the relationships between mathematics, the sciences, social studies, economics, and geography, as well as physical education and vocational education, are being reinforced by the integration of mathematical applications within these subjects. Consumer economics information, tax computations, stock market analyses, plus sports and other statistics that appear in the daily newspaper are some examples of real data that can be used in problem-solving. Students using minicalculators in real situations are reinforcing their own independent development of ideas.

Consumers as well as students are now armed with a tool that has enough power to compete effectively with the marketing techniques of the business community. With a minicalculator, students can help their parents save money by comparing unit prices, verifying bills and cash register tapes, and figuring discounts. Other applications outside the classroom include balancing checkbooks and family budgets, calculating income tax, computing gasoline mileage, converting U.S. to foreign currencies with their varying exchange rates, figuring tips, sharing dinner costs, and inventing and playing minicalculator games.[15]

Research Says

Teachers are experimenting extensively with minicalculators in their classrooms. Current reports proclaim increased interest in problem-solving through more relevant applications and improved attitudes towards mathematics.[16,17,18] While there

16

have been several brief minicalculator projects that produced very positive subjective evaluations and observations, as E. Glenadine Gibb points out in the Introduction to this report, the results of the limited research that are available have been inconclusive. Gaslin's studies[19] show that rote computational skills are significantly better when students use calculators. Cech[20] found that students learned to compute better with calculators than without them, and that using calculators has no effect on rote computational skills. Such conflicting results accentuate the immediate need for data based on longitudinal research which deals with the long-run impact of minicalculators. It is interesing to note that in 1955, experiments with desktop computing machines concluded that students gained in reasoning ability, computation ability, and interest in arithmetic while they learned more—machine computation plus ordinary arithmetic—in a machine-oriented environment.[21]

NCTM Involvement

In September 1974, the National Council of Teachers of Mathematics (NCTM) endorsed the minicalculator as a valuable instructional aid for mathematics education and recommended its use in the classroom by issuing the following position statement:

> With the decrease in cost of the minicalculator, its accessibility to students at all levels is increasing rapidly. Mathematics teachers should recognize the potential contribution of this calculator as a valuable instructional aid. In the classroom, the minicalculator should be used in imaginative ways to reinforce learning and to motivate the learner as he becomes proficient in mathematics.[22]

Recognizing such a statement as only a beginning, the NCTM Board of Directors at its September 1975 meeting approved a report from the Council's Instructional Affairs Committee (IAC) that identified nine ways in which the minicalculator can be used in the classroom:

1. To encourage students to be inquisitive and creative as they experiment with mathematical ideas
2. To assist the individual to become a wiser consumer
3. To reinforce the learning of basic number facts and properties in addition, subtraction, multiplication, and division
4. To develop the understanding of computational algorithms by repeated operations

5. To serve as a flexible "answer key" to verify the results of computation
6. To promote student independence in problem solving
7. To solve problems that previously have been too time consuming or impractical to be solved with paper and pencil
8. To formulate generalizations from patterns of numbers that are displayed
9. To decrease the time needed to solve difficult computations

The complete IAC report, including several examples for each statement, was published in the January 1976 issues of the *Arithmetic Teacher* and the *Mathematics Teacher,* the official journals of the NCTM. Additional minicalculator articles are featured in the November 1976 *Arithmetic Teacher.*

According to Dr. E. Glenadine Gibb, past president of the NCTM, "creative use, after the [mathematical] understandings have been extracted, can establish the calculator as a valuable asset in today's mathematics classroom."

A Minisurvey. As a part of a membership promotion in March 1975, the NCTM asked the mathematics department chairman of each public middle school and junior high school in the United States, "What's your position on the use of minicalculators in the classroom?" Seventy-two percent of the 103 respondents were in favor of using minicalculators. Their suggested uses for minicalculators extended the NCTM list, above, by one — assistance in teaching children with learning disabilities or handicaps.

They expressed concerns about the grade level appropriate for introducing minicalculators and about the potential effects of the minicalculator on testing and evaluation, on a person's ability to think, and on the learning of basic skills. Equal accessibility to minicalculators for all students, especially for students who cannot afford them, was also listed.

A Film Project. The NCTM, working with AESOP Films, Inc. of California, initially commissioned the production of a film designed to promote general public awareness of the educational value of minicalculators. During production, the project was expanded to three films as the result of a grant from National Semiconductor's NOVUS Consumer Products Division. The second and third films deal with using minicalculators to expand mathematics skills through classroom management and problem solving, respectively. Each 16-mm, color-and-sound film is twenty minutes long and has live action.

The distributor, Encyclopedia Britannica Education Corporation, has added three animated 16-mm films for students and a multimedia kit including five ten-minute sound films, 100 calculator-oriented task cards and a teacher's manual. Approximately \$250,000 has been invested in this cooperative venture.

Speakers. The NCTM, through its Instructional Affairs Committee, conventions, affiliated groups, and official journals, routinely identifies and shares imaginative ways of working with minicalculators. The titles of some presentations made at professional meetings include:

> *Using the Minicalculator to Teach Computation*
> *Teaching Algebra With the Aid of the Minicalculator*
> *Using the Minicalculator to Teach Problem Solving*
> *Choosing and Using Minicalculators*
> *The Minicalculator and Mathematics Instruction*
> *An Introduction to the Minicalculator*
> *Uses for Minicalculators in the High School Curriculum*

The NCTM Teacher/Learning Center. Acting as a communications network for the mathematics community, NCTM and NCTM Affiliated Group professional services regularly disseminate information concerning all facets of mathematics education. One of the newest resources is the Council's Teacher/Learning Center which is located in NCTM's headquarters in Reston, Virginia. Through the cooperation of other centers, Council members, and calculator manufacturers, a major collection of minicalculators and minicalculator information resources has been established at Reston. The free NCTM brochure entitled "Minicalculator Information Resources" was developed at the Center and made available in 1976.[23]

NACOME Recommendations

The Conference Board of the Mathematical Sciences appointed a National Advisory Committee on Mathematics Education (NACOME) in May 1974 to answer some of the questions being asked throughout the country as a result of declining student performance. With a grant from the National Science Foundation and funds for a national survey from the NCTM, the NACOME report may prove to be one of the most valuable contributions to mathematics education of the decade. The following statement is included among the final recommendations in the NACOME report (1975).

> At benchmark 1975 the National Advisory Committee on Mathematics Education sees the following recommendations as reasonable and essential features of a contemporary mathematics curriculum . . .
>
> > e) that beginning no later than the end of the eighth grade, a calculator should be available for each mathematics student during each mathematics class. Each student should be permitted to use the calculator during all of his or her mathematical work including tests.[24]

The NACOME report further states that "research is urgently needed concerning the uses of computing and calculating instruments in curriculum at all levels and their relationship to a broad array of instructional objectives"[25] and encourages "curricular revision or reorganization in the light of the increasing significance of computers and calculators."[26]

Other Activities

An example of a creative teacher using the minicalculator to improve student competencies and attitudes toward mathematics appeared in the May 1975 issue of *Mathematics in Michigan*. After Arthur W. Peterson provided his students with one of the variations of the "Shell Oil" inverted-display messages, his students started to bring in the series of articles which appear as the Appendix of this report. His implementation of this enjoyable teaching strategy shows what can happen as a result of bringing minicalculators into the classroom.[27]

At The Ohio State University in 1974, about 2600 students in a one-quarter remedial mathematics course purchased and used a basic minicalculator during the course, for all problem-solving, including tests. Although the instructors found their textbook somewhat inappropriate for use with minicalculators, they concluded that the minicalculator is an effective pedagogical tool for college mathematics.[28] Projects involving minicalculators are also being conducted at the University of Wisconsin-Madison, Indiana University, University of California-Berkeley, University of Denver, and Temple University.

A few calculator-based programs have appeared on the market. Publishers and other producers of instructional aids are developing and testing more programs. And this is just the beginning.

2. Implications and Conclusions

As minicalculators are used more extensively, we can expect significant changes that will strengthen the mathematics curriculum as we know it today. A process approach to learning may replace today's product-oriented programs. An understanding of mathematics may supplement getting-the-answers to problems. The emphasis may shift from computational speed as a measure of skill to consideration of the methods used in solving problems. By focusing on understanding, student competition for a teacher's approval based on providing "correct answers" may decrease and the understanding of concepts and computational algorithms may gain additional significance or relevance. However, drill will still be necessary to insure retention.

Methods of instruction will change, because the minicalculator can provide students with experiences that will accelerate and broaden their understanding of mathematical concepts and ideas. Teachers have already noted the impact of calculators on homework assignments.

Curriculum

Some changes that we can expect as calculators are integrated into the curriculum include the following:

1. Decimals will be introduced earlier, since minicalculators display fractions in decimal notation. There will be less work with common fractions; more with decimal frac-

tions. The study of rational numbers may accompany an earlier use of decimal notation. These may be among the first cha es in the mathematics curriculum, since they are also supported by metrication.

2. Negative numbers will appear earlier and more often, since minicalculators accept negative numbers as routinely as positive numbers.

3. Exponents, square roots, and large numbers will become part of the elementary curriculum.

4. Estimation, the concept of place value, significant digits, rounding-off skills, and mental arithmetic will take on new importance. Although minicalculators provide exact answers (when the input is correct), they do not give any indication as to the reasonableness of an answer.

5. Problem solving and problem analysis will receive greater emphasis. Prohibitive time-consuming computations will no longer inhibit learning.

6. Graphing will also receive greater emphasis. Since seeing is believing, minicalculators will aid in the understanding of complicated functions by allowing for more points to be identified within given time constraints.

7. Realism may be more readily displayed in the curriculum. Applications that rely on artificial problems with "convenient" numbers can be eliminated.

8. Interdisciplinary applications and activities encouraged by minicalculators may affect all academic levels as curriculum refinements continue.

9. Trigonometric and logarithmic functions may gain new importance as a result of time saved by use of minicalculators. The properties of these and other topics can be maximized as computation time is minimized. Since calculators can display specific table references on command, time spent on referring to tables and interpolation will be reduced.

10. Probability and statistics may be routinely incorporated into the curriculum.

11. Minicourses dealing with the different minicalculator logics should also be anticipated. (See Logic Systems p. 27.)

Inservice

The most important current aspect of minicalculators in education is the immediate need for inservice teacher education.

Guidelines for inservice programs should soon begin to appear in the professional literature as programs receive increased attention at the local level. While many educators have been engrossed with metrication programs, the calculators have appeared in the schools. As a result teachers are finding it necessary to develop an immediate working knowledge of these new instructional aids and their implications for education at the same time that they continue to play a major role in introducing the metric system as our new language of measurement.

Ideally, teachers should have hands-on experience with a variety of machines before introducing them into the classroom. The variety available today requires teachers to develop and maintain a continuing awareness of the capabilities of both old and new machines, and to know how to cope with hardware and software differences in the classroom. The demands placed on individual teachers will probably increase as they take on the responsibilities of a changing and expanding curriculum. Hence, they probably face a prolonged period of adjustment.

Questions that were previously discouraged will now be permitted, and calculations previously too complex and/or time-consuming are now feasible. This expansion of the curriculum will require that teachers maintain a continuing awareness of a broader range of topics. Of course, teachers are already adapting to these complexities as the number of students who own calculators continues to increase.

Classroom Management. New classroom management techniques will be required to maximize the use of calculators. Their power and flexibility may provide unique opportunities for teachers to respond to individual needs and they may also free the student from the constant attention of a teacher. Whether through mathematics laboratory activities, task cards, individual or group demonstrations or presentations, individual or team assignments, or enrichment activities, individualization can increase. The number of calculators in a classroom is not of primary importance. Activities can be designed to fit any situation. However, it is always advisable that *no more than* two students use one calculator at a time.

Classroom management techniques will also have to be developed to deal with the variety of machines being marketed today—with their different logics and degrees of sophistication—that may all appear in one classroom at the same time. The specialized calculator for use on an overhead projector and the talking calculator may be of some assistance. Of course a

23

classroom set of the same calculator model would help establish the ideal environment for using the minicalculator as an instructional aid.

Students

The minicalculator can serve all students. Liberated from computational drudgery, they are free to use their imaginations when confronted with new and varied problems, to progress faster and deal with more difficult problems, and to enjoy mathematics. Relevance, realism, significance, and experimentation will increase as students are free to test, sample, and investigate on their own. Students' career awareness may also increase as they find more applications for mathematics.

Slow Learners. We can expect minicalculators to provide slower students with confidence. When students with limited basic skills are freed from the tedium of performing manual calculations, they can concentrate on deciding when to add, subtract, multiply, and divide. Hopefully that possibility for decision-making will offer the kind of successful experiences that will give them the feeling of accomplishment and motivate them to develop their basic skills. Without computational frustration, students are able to develop a computational awareness that is conducive to critical thinking. Personalized instructional aids can motivate nonperformers to analyze and experiment.

Handicapped Students. The teaching of mentally, physically, and educationally handicapped students is another area for imaginative use of the minicalculator. Students who cannot write as fast as others (or cannot write at all)—but can think—will be freed from their physical limitations by the minicalculator.

There are even talking calculators designed for use by the blind.[1] Slower learners, the educationally handicapped, and even some mentally retarded students could benefit from using a talking calculator. Audio responses in languages other than English are already anticipated in future models.

Reading Difficulties. Since minicalculators can easily convert symbolic terms into their numerical equivalents, the reading difficulties attributed to the number of symbols used in mathematics may be reduced. It is much easier to cope with terms like $3\pi\sqrt{7}$, or $\sqrt[5]{17}$ as decimals, since it is easier to understand something when you have a feel for its size.

Discipline. Classroom discipline may even be affected by the minicalculator. With increased relevance afforded to all students by the individualized mathematical freedom of the minicalcula-

24

tors, interest in classroom activities could increase and discipline problems could decrease. With students accepting the additional responsibility of working with minicalculators and enjoying their use of minicalculators, the security concerns to prevent pilferage become minimal.[2]

Attitudes. The positive self-satisfaction provided by independent mathematical exploration may be able to counteract the negative, self-defeating attitudes toward mathematics that are so prevalent in our society today. If adults improve their attitudes toward computation and mathematics as a result of using minicalculators, young people may have an opportunity to enjoy mathematics without frequently hearing the undermining statement, "Oh, I've never been good at math either!" Thanks to current technology, today's students have a new opportunity to experience the power of mathematics and to enjoy mathematics. Maybe math topics will not produce instant anxiety for tomorrow's adults.

Testing and Evaluation

Minicalculators will significantly alter current testing and evaluation practices. Standardized testing programs may come to rely on the use of calculators. Eventually, mathematics tests utilizing minicalculators may be routinely used as instructional aids. Learning deficiencies can be more readily identified through diagnostic teaching with the help of minicalculators. Students can work more problems in less time, thereby generating more data for identifying difficulties.

There is nothing inherently wrong with making a mistake. Errors help us learn, and minicalculators will allow individuals to learn from their mistakes by allowing students time for experimentation to develop the correct solutions on their own. Since the curriculum should stress understanding, tests will have to be developed to better evaluate understanding. Testing and evaluation, then, becomes more productive, positive, and efficient.

Because of the calculator's speed, we will have to examine the role of time in testing. If time is a major factor in tests, then what knowledge are we testing? We might expect that, depending on the objectives of specific tests, for some the use of a calculator will be required and for others its use will be prohibited.

Equity. When minicalculators are used in testing and evaluation situations, the question of equity occurs immediately. Is it fair for those who own minicalculators to use them during examinations? Will allowing the students who own minicalculators to use them routinely in class, but not during examinations, handicap those students? Do students using minicalculators during examinations get better grades, since they can consider alternative solutions to problems in a relaxed manner without the same time constraints faced by students not using minicalculators? What if some students use more sophisticated calculators than other students?

While the minicalculator has made the slide rule an historical curiosity, the solutions to some of the equity problems will come from our experiences with slide rules. Schools could provide "basic" minicalculators for those students without them, and they should encourage students who own minicalculators to use them. This would be similar to the old slide rule policies.

Some critics are concerned that the use of minicalculators will further handicap students who have not developed minimum basic skills and who cannot afford to purchase minicalculators. They feel that minicalculators will discourage young people from acquiring basic mathematical skills, and therefore, they would be further isolated from the job market. While the concern is a very important one, there is no research to support this position.

In Conclusion

The use of minicalculators will never replace the need for understanding mathematical concepts, basic skills, or the teaching of mathematics. They will, however, increase the teacher's opportunities for providing insights into mathematics while increasing each school's academic responsibilities for providing an additional depth and breadth of topics within the existing curriculum, especially those related to the use of the minicalculator. An effort should be made to maximize the relationships between physical (pencil-and-paper and/or minicalculator) and mental mathematics through effective classroom presentations.

The public is warming up to mathematics—actually enjoying mathematics—because of minicalculators. Although it has long been socially acceptable to be poor in mathematics, people now are beginning to discuss computational games. The often frigid public attitude toward mathematics is warming up as more and more people use minicalculators. Let us hope that the day will come when it is socially acceptable in our culture to enjoy mathematics.

3. Selecting and Using Minicalculators

Before working with a minicalculator and trying some activities, we need to take a closer look at the calculator itself.

Logic Systems

Algebraic, RPN (Reverse Polish Notation), and arithmetic are the three different logic systems most frequently employed by minicalculators today.[1,2,3,4] Keycharts for the sample problem 5 − 4 ÷ 2 = 3 appear in figure 1. Variations of these systems with differing degrees of sophistication are also available.

The keyboard of a calculator with an algebraic logic system has an $\boxed{=}$ key and separate $\boxed{+}$ and $\boxed{-}$ keys. Since this allows the data to be entered as it is normally written, educators seem to prefer fully algebraic machines. However, many algebraic minicalculators do not follow the order-of-operations taught in the mathematics classroom. Some newer calculators are programmed to follow the standard algebraic rules and allow for varying levels of parentheses. Will your minicalculator display the correct answer when you enter the data as shown in the following keycharts?

$$8 \boxed{+} 2 \boxed{\times} 7 \boxed{=} \textbf{22. (not 70 or 14)}$$
$$85 \boxed{-} 15 \boxed{\div} 5 \boxed{=} \textbf{82. (not 14 or 3)}$$

The keyboard of a calculator employing RPN does not have

Figure 1

SAMPLE KEYCHARTS

LOGIC SYSTEMS

Algebraic

Texas Instruments, TI-30   5 [−] 4 [÷] 2 [=] **3.**

Novus, 832   4 [÷] 2 [CHS] [+] 5 [=] **3.**

Telesensory System, Speech +   4 [÷] 2 [=] [S] 5 [−] [S] [=] **3.00**

Omron, 88   4 [÷] 2 [+/−] 5 [=] **3.**

(The [CHS] and [+/−] keys change the sign of a number and the [S] key swaps the number displayed with the number in the memory.)

RPN (Reverse Polish Notation)

Novus, Mathematician   5 [ENT] 4 [ENT] 2 [÷] [−] **3.** or   4 [ENT] 2 [÷] [CHS] 5 [+] **3.**

Hewlett-Packard, H-P 21   5 [ENTER↑] 4 [ENTER↑] 2 [÷] [−] **3.**

Arithmetic

Sears   4 [÷] 2 [=] 5 [+] [=] **3.**

an $\boxed{=}$ key. RPN is a bracket-free logic system that many scientists and engineers prefer for advanced scientific applications. Minicourses dealing with RPN will probably be taught at the secondary level in the near future.

The keyboard of an arithmetic calculator features $\boxed{+}$ and $\boxed{=}$ keys. Although seldom found in newer minicalculators, this logic is commonly employed by desktop business machines.

Further investigation is encouraged. Remember identical keys on different machines may perform different functions.

Selecting a Minicalculator

After considering your current and future calculator needs and deciding on the logic system you prefer, identify and evaluate the following specific features before purchasing a minicalculator.

Review each machine's battery and AC adapter options. Compare the number of operating hours per battery or per charging. Automatic power-down and delayed power-off features insure the maximization of battery life. Charging batteries and contending with electrical cords can be tedious. Long-life replaceable batteries seem to be the most cost- and time-efficient.

Be sure that a calculator has a floating decimal point. To identify this feature, enter $7\boxed{\div}\boxed{9}\boxed{=}$. If **0.7777777** or **.7777777** is displayed on an eight-digit machine, the machine has a floating decimal point. If **0.7777778** or **.7777778** is displayed, the machine is programmed to round-off in the last place. Always be mindful of rounding-errors.

Display Considerations. Be sure that a minicalculator indicates an error when you divide by zero and/or indicates an overflow when you exceed the capacity of the machine. To check these features, enter $8\boxed{\div}\boxed{0}\boxed{=}$, 9999 $\boxed{y^x}$ 99 or 99999999 $\boxed{x^2}\boxed{x^2}\boxed{x^2}\boxed{x^2}$, and .01 $\boxed{y^x}$ 99 or .00000001 $\boxed{x^2}\boxed{x^2}\boxed{x^2}\boxed{x^2}$. Problems like $(999)^4 =$ _____ and $(.1)(.02)(.003)(.0004) =$ _____ can be used to evaluate most machines.

Remember to check for the machine's indication of a negative number. A negative sign should immediately precede a negative number.

Look for a calculator that has a bright, easily readable, eight-digit display with an acceptable viewing angle.

Other Considerations. In addition to selecting a calculator with the special keys and keyboard format you prefer, consider such options as memories, automatic constants (figure 2), programability, and print-outs and special functions like trigonometric, logarithmic, and hyperbolic. The manufacturer's manual is the best source of information for each model.

Select a reliable manufacturer that provides at least a twelve-month warranty and a repair service for its products. Most malfunctions occur during the first thirty days and are usually due to a power source failure.

Figure 2

AUTOMATIC CONSTANTS—preferably the last function and number entered before depressing the $\boxed{=}$ key.

KEYCHARTS for sample problems using a Litronix 2200.

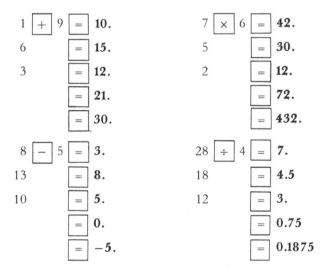

Keycharts

A keychart is the sequence of key symbols followed (with the machine display inserted as appropriate) when performing a specific computation on a minicalculator. Like flowcharts and computer programs, keycharts provide symbolic pathways to solving problems and are needed because the exactness demanded by computers is also needed for work with the calculator.

The notation for keycharting uses numerals for numbers; functions and special calculator keys are boxed; variables, unknowns, and blanks are indicated by a single underline; and calculator displays are indicated by a double underline when writing and are set in bold type for printed publications (figure 3). For each keychart, the calculator's logic, manufacturer, and model number should be identified. Keycharts can be written either horizontally or vertically (figure 4). Except where specifically noted, the keycharts in this report are for the algebraic Texas Instruments TI-30.

Some areas where keycharts can facilitate learning include the efficient analysis of complicated problems, alternative solutions to the same problem, solutions to a problem using different calculators, and new minicalculator algorithms (figure 5). Confidence in the minicalculator can increase through keycharting, since the user has a path to follow and steps to return to if distracted during a computation. Students and teachers will find that keycharting facilitates communications between the owners of different calculators. Teachers may rely on keycharting to evaluate student use of the minicalculator. While more than one keychart will produce the same result, the most efficient keychart will have the least number of entries for the machine used.

There are now and will be in the future other keychart formats for different applications. Educators are finding some minicalculator logic systems more appropriate than others for specific situations and grade levels. Ideas concerning these issues must receive immediate public attention so that acceptable standards can be considered for minicalculators, their logics, and keycharting.

Figure 3

Complete the following keycharts:

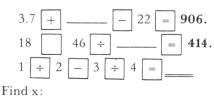

Find x:

893 ÷ x = **47.**   x = _____

x^2 + x − 6 = **14.**   x = _____

4. Activities

The activities on pages 35–53 may be transferred to activity cards for use with students in the classroom. Try them yourself beforehand, using your non-writing hand to operate your mini-calculator.

These activities were categorized by five graduate students at Virginia Polytechnic Institute, as follows:

> T—Time Saver
> R—Reinforcer
> M—Motivator
> C—Concept Developer
> S—Problem Solver (Applications)
> O—Other

The matrix in figure 6 (pages 50–53) summarizes their comments, suggestions, and categories for each activity.

NUMERATION & BASIC OPERATIONS

Correct these computations:

a.
```
   57
   46
 +213
 ────
  326
```
b.
```
   519
  -418
  ────
   111
```
c.
```
   61.49
 × 120.9
 ───────
 7432.93
```
d.
```
        83
127)10541
```

e. $1358 \div 28 = 48.6$ f. $974 \times 34 = 33\ 116$

Fill in the gaps ($\triangle$):

a.
```
  6 9 4 2
  1 △ △ △
+ 1 2 9 0
 ─────────
  10 2 0 0
```
b.
```
   4 △ △
 - △ 2 7
 ───────
   3 6 5
```
c.
```
      643
  × 128
  ─────
  5 △ 44
  12 △ 6
  64 △
 ───────
  82 △ 04
```

1
C

──────────────────────────────

FACTORIZATION

What are the prime factors of 90?

Keychart: 90 $\boxed{\div}$ 2 $\boxed{\div}$ **45.** 3 $\boxed{\div}$ **15.** 3 $\boxed{\div}$ **5.** 5 $\boxed{\div}$ **1.**

$90 = 2(3^2)(5)$ $\{2,3,5\}$

(Keycharts will vary with each minicalculator)

2
T

SOME PRACTICE

Display the following numbers:

a. 700   b. 5123   c. 123456   d. 809   e. 2.54   f. 0.13

Keychart

Generate the following sequences: Algebraic, UNITREX 80 M

a. 2, 4, 6, 8, 10, 12, ...   2 [+] [+] ...

b. 3, 6, 9, 12, 15, 18, ...   3 [+] [+] ...

c. 2, 4, 8, 16, 32, 64, ...   2 [×] [×] ...

d. 5, 0, −5, −10, −15, −20, ...   5 [+] [−] [−] ...

e. 2, 1., .5, .25, .125, .0625, ...   2 [÷] [÷] ...

What is the largest number that can be displayed on your mini-calculator? _____

(Keycharts will vary with each minicalculator)

3

INTRODUCTORY MINICALCULATOR
COMMUNICATIONS

Enter . 7 7 3 4 and rotate your machine 180° for a greeting.

- -

The little green sprout exclaimed 9 1 8 5 . 3 4, when he first saw the jolly green giant (JGG).

To find out how the JGG responded (to four decimal places); [+] 7 . 4 1 7 5 to the exclamation; [×] by 1 . 0 9 6 3; [−] 9 8 7 6 ; and [÷] by 5 0 0

(Minicalculator used—LITRONIX 2200)

XMAS MINICALCULATOR COMMUNICATIONS

1. Santa's reindeer wear 5 7 7 3 8.   Keychart

2. Why does Santa get stuck in so   Algebraic, UNITREX 80M
   many chimneys?

   a. Start with your Christmas
      savings ($33.50),   3   3   .   5   0

   b. Divide by the number of people
      in your family (4),   ÷   4 = +

   c. Subtract the number of red-
      nosed reindeer,   1   −

   d. Multiply by the number of
      regular reindeer,   ×   8   =

   e. Divide by twice the number of
      partridges in a peartree,   ÷   2   =

   f. Multiply by the number of
      "Days of Christmas" in
      1000 years,   ×   1   2   000   = [

   g. Subtract the bicentennial
      number,   2   0   0   −

   h. Add the price of a small gift
      ($5.34).   5   .   3   4   +

   (Keycharts will vary with each minicalculator)

MINICALCULATOR COMMUNICATIONS

Given: 0 = O

1 = I

3 = E

4 = H

5 = S

7 = L

8 = B

9 = G

. = 0 (when words end in 0, the decimal point must be depressed first)

–and–

the "ability" to rotate a minicalculator 180°.

Create your own messages.

1. By direct display entries

-or-

2. By calculations

6
M

BONUS QUESTIONS

1. Is the zipcode for the NCTM headquarters office (22091) a prime number?

2. How many seconds are there in one year (365 days)?

3. $\sqrt{13} = 13^{1/2}$ True or False?

4. $53^{-1} = 1/53$ True or False?

5. Is your zipcode a prime number?

7

SIMPLIFY

Use your minicalculator to simplify the following expressions in as few steps as possible.

EXAMPLE: $7^2 + 4^2 = \mathbf{65}$.   Keychart: 7 $\boxed{x^2}$ $\boxed{+}$ 4 $\boxed{x^2}$ $\boxed{=}$ 65.

1. 2^5

2. $(\frac{4}{7})^2$

3. $(.4)^7$

4. $(6.4)^4$

5. $(8\frac{1}{3})^3$

6. 3×7^2

7. $13^2 + 9^3$

8. $17^3 - 5^4$

9. $(7 - 3 \times 4)^2$

10. $\dfrac{12^2 + 7^5 + 5^4}{6}$

(Keycharts will vary with each minicalculator)

ORDERED PAIRS

Given that x and y are members of the set of real numbers, generate twenty ordered pairs with your minicalculator that can be used to graph the functions defined by the following equations.

1. $y = x^2$

2. $y = 3x^3$

3. $y = -5x^2$

4. $y = x^4 + 3$

5. $y = x^2 + 2x - 8$

HAVING A PARTY?

Joe is having a pizza party for his friends. He is going to order 5 of each of the following pizzas from the Bocce Club Pizzeria. How much will the pizza for the party cost?

PIZZA	COST	SUBTOTALS
Cheese	$1.60	_____
Cheese and Pepperoni	$2.00	_____
Cheese and Mushroom	$2.15	_____
Double Cheese	$2.30	_____
Cheese and Sausage	$2.40	_____
Cheese and Shrimp	$2.70	_____
	TOTAL COST:	[ ]

10
S

EARN YOUR MONEY

Tom is a handyman. Last week he worked on Monday: for 8 hours at $3.25 per hour; Tuesday: for 9 hours at $3.50 per hour; Wednesday: for 7 hours at $2.75 per hour; Thursday: for 7.5 hours at $4.25 per hour; and Friday: he earned $51.80. How much did he earn?

Monday	_____
Tuesday	_____
Wednesday	_____
Thursday	_____
Friday	_____
TOTAL EARNINGS:	[ ]

11
S

COMMISSIONS

Given:

1. A daily base salary of $15; and
2. 4% commission on the first $300 in sales;
   5% commission on sales over $300 but less than $500;
   6% commission on sales over $500.

What are the total earnings of a salesperson who sells $750.00 worth of products in one day?

12
S

CAR CALCULATIONS

Given that each stop for gasoline is a fill-up; completing the chart below will provide regular MPG data. Fluctuations in MPG reflect changing driving conditions as well as variations in automobile performance. (With increasing oil costs, it's probably a good idea to check the accuracy of your "friendly" gas pump.)

DATE	MILEAGE	MILEAGE BETWEEN FILL-UPS	GALLONS	MILES/GALLON

13
S

NEWSPAPER ADVERTISING

Using the classified ad section of a newspaper and the rate schedule published in that section or that is available from the newspaper's office:

1. Determine the cost of an ad if it is to run for 1 day; 5 days; 7 days; and 10 days.
2. Determine the average cost per line for each case.
3. Determine the average cost per word for each case.
4. Select three other ads. Determine the cost for each ad if they are run for 1 day; 5 days; and 10 days. Determine the total cost of running all three ads for the same time periods.

14
S

ADDITION NIM FOR PARTNERS

Take turns adding 1, 2, or 3 to the number displayed on your minicalculator; starting with 0. The first person displaying 21 wins.

15
M

SUBTRACTION NIM FOR PARTNERS

Take turns subtracting 1, 2, or 3 from the number displayed on your minicalculator; starting with 21. The first person displaying 0 wins.

16
M

SOME MORE PRACTICE

Fill in the missing numbers:

5, 25, 125, ---, 3125, 15 625, ...
4, 16, ---, 65 536, ...

Beginning with 0, find the 11th even number.

17
C

MULTIPLICATION

1. Compute 7 × 476 without using the $\boxed{\times}$ key. Check by using the $\boxed{\times}$ key.

   Keychart:

2. Compute 137 × 476 without using the $\boxed{\times}$ key. Check by using the $\boxed{\times}$ key.

   Keychart:

(Hint—consider expanded notation.)

(Keycharts will vary with each minicalculator)

18
R, C

PATTERNS

1. $\dfrac{10}{81} =$

   $\dfrac{1000}{891} =$

   $\dfrac{1000}{8991} =$

   $\dfrac{10\,000}{89\,991} =$

2. $\dfrac{500}{499} =$

   $\dfrac{1000}{999} =$

   $\dfrac{1000}{997} =$

   $\dfrac{1000}{996} =$

   $\dfrac{10\,000}{9999} =$

19
M

45

"GUESS—TIMATION"

$$\boxed{}^5 = 161\ 051$$

$$\sqrt[3]{12\ 812\ 904} = \boxed{}$$

$$\boxed{}^4 = 707\ 281$$

$$\sqrt{39} = 6\ .\ \underline{}\ \underline{}\ \underline{}$$

20
T

COMPARE, WHAT, HOW MANY TIMES?

Add 1234 eight times. Compare this sum with the product of 1234 × 8.

What number multiplied by itself will generate 4489 as a product?

How many times can 17 be subtracted from 1513? Check your answer by division. Without using the $\boxed{\div}$, solve 4128 ÷ 258.

21
C

PARTNERSHIP PRACTICE

Use the minicalculator to practice basic skills.

One student states a basic fact like (3×7), $(23 - 4)$, $(15 \div 3)$, or $(17 + 5)$; then uses the minicalculator to compute the answer.

The other student writes the answer or responds verbally; recording the number of correct and incorrect answers as verified by the first student.

The students then switch positions, process the same number of problems, and compare records.

22
R

THE ANSWER KEY

Use your minicalculator as a flexible answer key to check the following computations. Correct any incorrect answers.

$$264\overline{)440.88} = 1.67 \qquad 871.3\overline{)11\ 675.42} = 13.4$$

$$\begin{array}{r} 19.76 \\ \times\ 123.4 \\ \hline 2348.834 \end{array} \qquad \begin{array}{r} 9876 \\ \times\ 34.15 \\ \hline 373265.4 \end{array}$$

23
R

TARGETS FOR PARTNERS

A multiplication game for two people where one persons picks a target and the other selects a constant multiplier. Take turns at guessing the other factor and verify your guess with the minicalculator.

EXAMPLE: Target = 735   Constant = 15

24
M

SOME PROBLEMS

Use your minicalculator to verify and correct the following statements:

1. Eight toys at $1.13 a piece will cost $9.14.

2. The interest on $7500 at 7.5% for 9 months is $421.88.

25
R, S

EXERCISE

What is 8! ?

$$1! = 1$$
$$2! = 1 \times 2$$
$$3! = 1 \times 2 \times 3$$

Find the $\sqrt[3]{9}$ by successive approximations.

Compare the values of $(3^2)^4$ and 3^{2^4}.

26
T, C

Figure 6

Card Number	Students					Dominant Category(ies)	Comments and Suggestions
	I	II	III	IV	V		
1	C	M,C	O	T	C	C	(III) Some easier w/o a calculator; Good practice; (IV) Orientation—any level
2	T	T,C	T	R	R,M C,S	T	(III) Grade 8; (IV) Grades 7,8; (V) Maybe better to say "Verify the prime factors of 90"
3	C	M	O	S	R,M C,S		(III) Familiarization; (IV) Orientation— grades 7,8
4	M	M	M	M	M	M	(III) Difficult to figure out; (IV) Elementary; (V) Who explains upside down "hello"
5	M	M,S	M	M	M	M	(III) Difficult to figure out; (IV) Kids will not know answers to questions—provide answers

#	M	—	M	M	M	M	Comments
6	T	C	—	R	M,S		(II) Don't understand; (III) Fun for any grade level; (IV) Any age
7	C	·	T,R	T	M,S		(I) Replace w/: Is your zipcode a prime?; (III) Tedious; (IV) Grades 7,8; (V) What is NCTM?
8	C	T,R	T,R	T	M,C / S	T	(III) Excellent example; (IV) Knowledge of powers very helpful
9	T	T	T,R	S	M,C / S	T	(III) Twenty ordered pairs too many; Great for algebra II students; (IV) Grade 8 or algebra
10	S	S	S	T,S	T,M / C,S	S	(III) Good for most grade levels; (IV) Elementary up
11	S	S	S	T,S	T,M / C,S	S	(III) Good applications; (IV) Elementary up
12	S	S	T,R / S	S	T,M / C,S	S	(III) Grade 8; (IV) Grades 6,7,8

Figure 6 (continued)

Card Number	Students					Dominant Category(ies)	Comments and Suggestions
	I	II	III	IV	V		
13	S	T,R	M,S	S	T,M C,S	S	(III) Excellent reason for anyone to own a calculator; (IV) Consumer math
14	S	S	S	S	T,M C,S	S	(III) Good problem; (IV) Could not find rate schedule
15	M	M	M	C	M	M	(III) Good for younger children; (IV) Elementary up
16	M	M	M	C	M	M	(III) Good for younger children; (IV) Elementary up
17	C	T	—	S	M,C	C	(III) Don't understand 2d line; (IV) "Beginning"—Mean place 0 in calculator then count 11 even #s or is 0 1st even #?
18	C	C	R	R	R,M C	R,C	(III) 1st exercise good to reinforce meaning of multi.; 2d too tedious; (IV) Difficult problem; (V) May not be clear to all
19	R	T	M	M	M,S	M	(III) Very interesting; (IV) Very interesting—elementary up

20	T	T	C	M	T,M C,S	T	(III) Calculator very valuable here; (IV) Grades 7,8
21	C	R,C	R,C	T,R	T,M C,S	C	(III) Meaning of multiplication and division great!; (IV) Grades 6,7
22	R	M	R,M	R	T,R M,S	R	(III) Good interest stimulator; (IV) Elementary and remedial
23	T,R	R	R	M	T,R M	R	(IV) Elementary up; orientation
24	C	M	M	M,S	R,M C	M	(IV) Grades 7,8
25	S	R	R	S	T,M	R,S	(III) Good—shows usefulness; (IV) Grades 6,7
26	C	C	T	S	T,R M	T,C	(IV) Grades 7,8

References

Chapter One — The Age of the Minicalculator

1. Delaney, William, "Pocket Calculators — Boom Adds Up to Controversy." *The Washington Star,* November 10, 1975.
2. Caravella, Joseph R., *A Consumer's Guide to Minicalculators.* Washington D.C., National Education Association, 1976.
3. Leitzel, Joan, and Bert Waits, "Hand Held Calculators in the Freshman Mathematics Classroom." Unpublished paper, Ohio State University, February 1975.
4. Wehner, Carl, "Pocket Calculators in the Classroom." Iowa Council of Teachers of Mathematics, *I.C.T.M. Journal* 4, Fall 1975: 22–25.
5. Immerzeel, George, "It's 1986 and Every Student Has a Calculator." *Instructor* 85, April 1976: 46–51 and 148.
6. Judd, Wallace P., "A New Case for the Calculator." *Learning* 3, 1975: 41–48.
7. Leitzel, Joan, and Bert Waits, "Hand Held Calculators in the Freshman Mathematics Classroom." Unpublished paper, Ohio State University, February 1975.
8. Parks, Terry E., "Mini-Calculators: Opportunity or Dilemma." Kansas Association of Teachers of Mathematics *Bulletin* 49, April 1975: 18–20.
9. Wehner, Carl, "Pocket Calculators in the Classroom." Iowa Council of Teachers of Mathematics, *I.C.T.M. Journal* 4, Fall 1975: 22–25.
10. Immerzeel, George, "It's 1986 and Every Student Has a Calculator." *Instructor* 85, April 1976: 46–51 and 148.
11. Hawthorne, Frank S., "Hand-Held Calculators: Help or Hindrance?" *Arithmetic Teacher* 20, December 1973: 671–72.
12. Hawthorne, Frank S., and John J. Sullivan, "Using Hand-Held Calculators in Sixth Grade Mathematics Lessons." *New York State Mathematics Teachers' Journal* 25, January 1975: 29–31.
13. Del Seni, Donald L., "Use of Hand Calculators in Mathematics Instruction." Association of Teachers of Mathematics of New York City, *Summation* 21, Fall 1975: 5–6.
14. Wehner, Carl, "Pocket Calculators in the Classroom." Iowa Council of Teachers of Mathematics, *I.C.T.M. Journal* 4. Fall 1975: 22–25.
15. Caravella, Joseph R., *A Consumer's Guide to Minicalculators.* Washington, D.C., National Education Association, 1976.
16. Del Seni, Donald L., "Use of Hand Calculators in Mathematics Instruction." Association of Teachers of Mathematics of New York City, *Summation* 21, Fall 1975: 5–6.
17. Immerzeel, George, "It's 1986 and Every Student Has a Calculator." *Instructor* 85, April 1976: 46–51 and 148.
18. Leitzel, Joan, and Bert Waits, "Hand Held Calculators in the Freshman Mathematics Classroom." Unpublished paper, Ohio State University, February 1975.
19. Gaslin, William L., "A Comparison of Achievement and Attitudes

of Students Using Conventional or Calculator-Based Algorithms for Operations on Positive Rational Numbers in Ninth Grade General Mathematics." *Journal for Research in Mathematics Education* 6, March 1975: 95–108.

20. Cech, Joseph R., "The Effect of the Use of Desk Calculators on Attitude and Achievement with Low-Achieving Ninth Graders." *Mathematics Teacher* 65, February 1972: 183–86.

21. Fehr, Howard F., George McMeen, and Max Sobol, "Using Hand-Operated Computing Machines in Learning Arithmetic." *Arithmetic Teacher* 3, October 1956: 145–50.

22. National Council of Teachers of Mathematics, "NCTM Board Approves the Use of Minicalculators in the Mathematics Classroom." *Newsletter* 11, December 1974: 3.

23. National Council of Teachers of Mathematics, "Minicalculator Information Resources." January 1976.

24. National Advisory Committee on Mathematical Sciences (NACOME), *Overview and Analysis of School Mathematics Grades K-12.* Washington, D.C.: Conference Board of Mathematical Sciences, 1975: 138.

25. *Ibid.,* 144.

26. *Ibid.,* 145.

27. Peterson, A. W., "Calculated Class Madness." Michigan Council of Teachers of Mathematics, *Mathematics in Michigan* 14, May 1975: 18–23.

28. Leitzel, Joan, and Bert Waits, "Hand Held Calculators in the Freshman Mathematics Classroom." Unpublished paper, Ohio State University, February 1975.

Chapter Two —Implications and Conclusions

1. Thornton, Carol A., "Measure Up Via Calculator Skills." Illinois State University, *Math Lab Matrix* 5, Spring 1975: 3.

2. Del Seni, Donald L., "Use of Hand Calculators in Mathematics Instruction." Association of Teachers of Mathematics of New York City, *Summation* 21, Fall 1975: 5–6.

Chapter Three — Selecting and Using Minicalculators

1. Readers' Dialogue. *Arithmetic Teacher* 22, December 1975: 158–60.

2. Beakley, George C. and H. W. Leach. *The Slide Rule, Electronic Hand Calculator, and Metrification in Problem Solving,* 3rd ed. New York: Macmillan Publishing Co., 1975.

3. Caravella, Joseph R. *A Consumer's Guide to Minicalculators.* Washington D.C., National Education Association, 1976.

4. "Calculators." *Consumer Reports,* September 1975: 533–41.

Appendix

1. I work for the United States government. I travel 100,000 miles a year. Multiply this by the number of top officials around the world that I negotiate with, which is 531; add the $70,000 I get paid by underground and top companies throughout the world and the $7,735 I receive from the U.S. Government. I work with the CIA. What is my function?

Brad Bond
Mark Grost

2. Little Marvin Peabody went skiing in the Rocky Mountains. Unfortunately, Marvin's vacation was cut short when he broke a bone. To find out what bone he broke, do the following on your calculator. Take the 48 kids in Marvin's 2nd grade class and multiply this by the 10,000 ski lodges in the U.S. Add to this the 7,623 people in Marvin's town. Substract from this the 168,866 skiing injuries per year in the U.S. Multiply this by the two times President Ford wiped out on his recent skiing trip. Now turn your calculator over and you will know what bone Marvin broke!

Tom Wilkie

3. OK, calculator fans: today, we are going to discuss our lovable President Gerald R. Ford. He is without a doubt the best President we have had since Nixon, but he does have one annoying fault. To find out what it is, do the following on your calculator. Take the 50,000 members of Ford's Cabinet and multiply this by the 6 of them that actually earn their pay. From this total subtract the 73,648 relatives of his cabinet that are also on the government payroll. Add to this the 39,515 that is the average salary of each of these people. Now multiply this total by 2, which is the average number of times that Listerine lasts longer than the leading mouthwash, when President Ford uses it. Now turn your calculator upside down, and you will see what Ford's main problem is!

Tom Wilkie

4. Everyone knows that Ford's ideas (Ford had a better idea) often go down to dismal defeat in Congress. To find out what our Captain America says when this happens, get out your calculator (or Mr. Peterson's) and do the following: First, enter 710,

which when the calculator is turned over, is the biggest problem of the Ford Administration. Then multiply by the $3.00 tax which Ford wanted to put on each barrel of this precious substance. Add 120, which is the number of times that he played football without his helmet in college. Divide by 5 which is the average number of headaches he gets a day. Multiply by 10, which is the average number of Excedrin tablets a day. Now add 6 which is his average on a par 4 golf hole and . . . you will have Ford's expression of defeat. Tom Wilkie, eat your heart out!!!

Stan Hatch

5.   All you calculator fans have probably noticed a competition building up between me and Stanley Hatch. He ended his latest "calculator story" with "Tom Wilkie, eat your heart out." Now I don't want to start a verbal battle of wits, because that would leave Stan unarmed. But I do want a chance to express my side of the story. So, if you do the following on your calculator, the result will be my opinion of Stan Hatch!

First of all take 100 (Stanley's favorite number*) and multiply this by the 240,000 times he has received them this year. Add the 268,869 theorems he has memorized and divide this by the 3 times he has ever spent more than ten seconds on a proof. From this total, subtract the 14,010 proofs he has done this year, and add the 5 proofs that have been wrong. (Heaven forbid.) Now turn your calculator over, and you will see, Stan Hatch, you are a ....!

Tom Wilkie

6.   Now, now boys enough of this bickering. For two people to continue fighting this way takes something special in their heads. To find out what you two have take the St. Johns first 3 phone numbers 224 and add 26,020 which is the actual number of theorems that Stan has memorized. Add Tom's average which is 99. To this figure add Tom's and Stan's I.Q.'s together which total 200. When you multiply everything by two, which is the number of people fighting (Tom and Stan) add 618. Turn your calculator upside down and read. Now push "=" and you get what you both have lots of in your heads. Next time you boys want another lesson let me know.

Dwayne Dush

*T.N. Also his average on Geometry Tests

7. Dear Mr. Wilkie:

It has come to my attention that on March 13 (Enter 313) you publicly declared me a big slob. I deny this. Now not only am I not big, I am also not a slob, in my humble opinion. To find out what I think you should do, do the following on the calculator: To the 313 already entered, multiply by 43, which is the number of times it takes you to correctly tie your shoes on an average morning. To this, add 47, your share of the combined I.Q. that Dwayne Dush mentioned. From this subtract 6,398, the true number of theorems (to set the record straight), I have memorized. Press "=" and you will have the 1st part of what you should do. Press it again and you will have the last part. _____ in _____ . And as for you Dwayne Dush, Mind Your Own Business!

Stan Hatch

8. As all of you know by now, Stan is getting a little violent in the "calculator war." In his latest message he threatened to boil me in oil. This proves what a crude person he is. Here we are in the middle of an "energy crisis" and he wants to waste good oil like that. To find out what I think of his plan in general, do the following on your calculator: Take 1, which is the number of theorems I have memorized and subtract 0.9 which is Dwayne's I.Q. (He was too modest to mention it.) Now multiply this by the age of 8, which is Stan's current mental level. Divide by the 2 feet of Dwayne's height and add 0.00404 in. which is the length of the longest hair on Dwayne's head. Now push "=" down, this is my initial reaction to Stan's threat. As for you Dwayne Flush, you figure this out! Since you're so weak minded, I'll make it easy for you, just enter 7,718,618 on the calculator and turn it upside down. In other words, keep your _____ _____ out of my business!

T. Wilkie

9. I have tried to be a nice guy by trying to get you two to stop fighting. The gratitude I get is to keep my _____ _____ out of your business. Now that you have pointed this out, I want to tell you how I feel. Compute the number of tears I cried over this which is 667. Add the degree of anger and hostility you have, 3,000. Multiply by the people ganging up on me and push "=." When you turn the calculator upside down you will see that I feel like a _____ . Now clear your calculators and I will tell you what I think you two are. Take my I.Q. (since I have gotten

over my modesty) which is .9, add my pencil length of 1.1. Multiply by 189,403 because that is the total of 4th hours' favorite numbers and push the "=." Pronounce the word you read twice out loud, and every one will know what you both are.

Dwayne Dush

10. Good Grief! Or, as Jerry Ford would say, "Gosh!" I have never seen two more spoiled brats in my entire life. I make one little comment about our "fearful leader" President Ford, and Stanley jumps all over me and threatens to boil me in oil, among other crude things. And then Dwayne sticks his royal schnozola into it, and when he is told to mind his own bees wax, he cries (by his own admission), 667 tears. What a baby! Bet there is a better word that covers both Stan and Dwayne. To find out what this word is, break out the calculators, boys!

First, take 100,000, my I.Q. (I've gotten over my modesty, too!). Multiply this by the 8 digits on this calculator. From this, subtract the 160,249 members of the Tom Wilkie Fan Club (Mid-Michigan Chapter). Add to this the 25,000 students and teachers at St. Johns High who have tried these "calculator doodles" by now, and multiply by the 16 that have managed to understand them. Divide this by the 2 people in this war who have made any sense. (Me and myself.) Press the "=" button, turn the calculator upside down (if you are able) and you will see the answer. Dwayne and Stan, you are a couple of big ———— !

Tom Wilkie

11. Dwayne, Stan, and Tom:

Having fun fighting? Well I also have an opinion of all of you, which you can find by doing the following: Enter .918, turned over is what none of you are but is part of the answer. Next add 2.39, your 3 combined I.Q.'s and divide by Stan's real number of memorized theorems which is 10. Next multiply by 3 (number fighting before I came) and add .0002 because I am equal to two of you. Now multiply by 5 (number now fighting—you 3 and my 2) and add .7704. Before you press "equal," turn it upside down and read the second word. When you press equal you will read the third word. Your brains are in your ———— ———— ————.

Gerald Good

12. Let's get our calculators out again just for fun. Let's call this fight a game. Rules are: the loser of this calculator fight is the winner of this game. So let's start with the common phrase,

0.7734 to all. Now multiply by 5, number fighting (remember?). Now add a St. John's phone number, let's say, 2247.133 all of us are so modest, so why don't I just for awhile, put me down to your level. So for the next number let's take the first 2 that started fighting plus Dwayne plus me = 4. So subtract 2114. For the next number multiply by the number of brains involved 8, 2 each, sorry to say that one of yours is lost and the other is looking for it. So that leaves my two working and they don't have to work very hard. Let's add 3410, when you push equal, you get Tom's and Ford's famous word. Multiply times 719, number of mistakes Dwayne makes in a week. Now add 2346, our I.Q.'s total, let's not be modest, we're all smart. Now divide by the second row .456, now add 604, before pushing equal, turn it upside down, this is part of the name, now push equal, the name of the game is _____ on the _____ .

Gerald Good

13.   Once upon a time, there were 2 nations that just kept on fighting. Then another country got into it and then another and then it was World War I. Tom, I think that the 2 of us should unite and wipe out those 2 slobs. To find out what those 2 have lots of in their heads, do the following: First take .5 because you're both half-wits and add 1, the number of people in the Gerald Good Fan Club nationwide (himself). Now, multiply by 100, my favorite number*. Subtract 8, Dwayne's favorite number and multiply by 10, Gerald's favorite number. Add 1, the highest number Dwayne ever counted up to without using his fingers and multiply by 5 (their brains are equal to 5% of mine). Now, all that remains is to press "=" even though none of you will ever equal me. Now when the calculator is turned upside down you can see what you have lots of in your head. I hope I've taught you to mind your own business!!

Stan Hatch

*Average on Geometry tests

Bibliography

ASCD News Exchange "Use of Hand Calculators in Schools Widens, a Few Still Urge Caution." 17 (May 1975): 8.

Beakley, George C., and H. W. Leach. *The Slide Rule, Electronic Hand Calculator, and Metrification in Problem Solving.* 3rd ed. New York: Macmillan Publishing Co. 1975.

Berger, I. "Calculators Get Smaller, Smarter and Cheaper." *Popular Mechanics,* December 1974: 70–75 and 168.

Bolder, Jacqueline. "Calculator Use Doesn't Add Up, Md. NAACP Says." *The Washington Star* 26 October 1975.

"Calculation or Computation? Is that the Question?" *Teacher* 92 (March 1975): 52.

Caravella, Joseph R. *A Consumer's Guide to Minicalculators.* Washington, D.C. National Education Association, 1976.

Cech, Joseph R. "The Effect of the Use of Desk Calculators on Attitude and Achievement with Low-Achieving Ninth Graders." *Mathematics Teacher* 65, February 1972: 183–86.

Consumer Reports, "Calculators." September 1975: 533–41.

Consumer Reports. "Electronic Mini Calculators." June 1973: 372–77.

D'Aulaire, Emily, and Ola D'Aulaire. "Put a Computer in Your Pocket." *Reader's Digest,* September 1975: 115–18.

Del Seni, Donald L. "Use of Hand Calculators in Mathematics Instruction." (Association of Teachers of Mathematics of New York City) *Summation* 21, Fall 1975: 5–6.

Delaney, William. "Pocket Calculators—Boom Adds Up to Controversy." *The Washington Star,* 10 November 1975.

Fehr, Howard F., George McMeen, and Max Sobol. "Using Hand-Operated Computing Machines in Learning Arithmetic." *Arithmetic Teacher* 3, October 1956: 145–50.

Free, John R. "Now—There's a Personal Calculator for Every Purse and Purpose." *Popular Science,* February 1975: 78–81 and 136.

Gaslin, William L. "A Comparison of Achievement and Attitudes of Students Using Conventional or Calculator-Based Algorithms for Operations on Positive Rational Numbers in Ninth Grade General Mathematics." *Journal for Research in Mathematics Education* 6, March 1975: 95–108.

Gibb, E. Glenadine. "Calculators in the Classroom." *Today's Education,* November/December 1975: 42–44.

Gilbert, Jack. *Advanced Applications for Pocket Calculators.* Blue Ridge Summit, Pennsylvania: TAB Books, 1975.

Hawthorne, Frank S. "Hand-Held Calculators: Help or Hindrance?" *Arithmetic Teacher* 20, December 1973: 671–72.

Hawthorne, Frank S., and John J. Sullivan. "Using Hand-Held Calculators in Sixth Grade Mathematics Lessons." *New York State Mathematics Teachers' Journal* 25, January 1975: 29–31.

Hoffman, Ruth I. "Don't Knock the Small Calculator—Use It!" *Instructor* 85, August/September: 149–50.

Huff, D. "Teach Your Pocket Calculator New Tricks to Make Life Simpler." *Popular Science,* December 1974: 96–98 and 118–19.

Hunter, William L. *Getting the Most Out of Your Electronic Calculator.* Blue Ridge Summit, Pennsylvania: TAB Books, 1974.

Immerzeel, George. "It's 1986 and Every Student Has a Calculator." *Instructor* 85, April 1976: 46–51 and 148.

Jefimenko, Oleg D. *How to Entertain with Your Pocket Calculator.* Star City, W. Virginia: Electret Scientific Co., 1975.

Judd, Wallace P. "A New Case for the Calculator." *Learning* 3, 1975: 41–48.

Judd, Wallace P. *Games, Tricks, and Puzzles for a Hand Calculator.* Menlo Park California: Dymax, 1974.

Leitzel, Joan, and Bert Waits. "Hand Held Calculators in the Freshman Mathematics Classroom." Unpublished paper, Ohio State University, February 1975.

Machlowitz, Eleanore. "Electronic Calculators — Friend or Foe of Instruction?" *Mathematics Teacher* 69, February 1976: 104–106.

Mathematics Student 22, December 1974: 1–2. "Santa Takes a Calculated Risk."

McKellips, Terral. "What Are We Going to Do About Calculators?" *The Oklahoma Council of Teachers of Mathematics Newsletter,* Fall 1974: 4–5.

Myrick, Alvin G. "Electronic Calculators in School Mathematics." (North Carolina Council of Teachers of Mathematics) *Centroid* 1, Spring 1975: 4–6.

National Advisory Committee on Mathematical Sciences (NACOME). *Overview and Analysis of School Mathematics Grades K–12.* Washington, D.C.: Conference Board of Mathematical Sciences, 1975: 24–25, 34, 40–43, 138, 141, 144–145.

National Association of Secondary School Principals. *Curriculum Report* 4, October 1975.

National Council of Teachers of Mathematics. "Minicalculator Information Resources," January 1976.

National Council of Teachers of Mathematics. "NCTM Board Approves the Use of Minicalculators in the Mathematics Classroom." *Newsletter* 11, December 1974: 3.

NCTM Instructional Affairs Committee. "Minicalculators in Schools." *Mathematics Teacher* 69, January 1976.

Parks, Terry E. "Mini-Calculators: Opportunity or Dilemma." Kansas Association of Teachers of Mathematics *Bulletin* 49, April 1975: 18–20.

Peterson, A. W. "Calculated Class Madness." Michigan Council of Teachers of Mathematics, *Mathematics in Michigan* 14, May 1975: 18–23.

Readers' Dialogue. *Arithmetic Teacher* 22, December 1975: 158–60.

Reeves, Charles A. "Planning to Use Calculators?" Texas Council of Teachers of Mathematics, *Texas Mathematics Teacher* 22, October 1975: 3–4.

Roberts, Edward M. *Fingertip Math.* Dallas: Texas Instruments, Inc. 1974.

Rogers, James T. *The Calculating Book: Fun and Games with Your Pocket Calculator.* New York: Random House, 1975.

Skoll, Pearl A. *Coping with the Calculator.* Northridge, California: Pearl A. Skoll, 1975.

Stultz, Lowell. "Electronic Calculators in the Classroom." *Arithmetic Teacher* 22, February 1975: 135–38.

Sutz, Sherilyn P. "Calculator Center." Kansas Association of Teachers of Mathematics, *Bulletin* 49, April 1975: 20–21.

Teacher 92, March 1975: 52, "Calculation or Computation? Is that the Question?"

Thornton, Carol A. "Measure Up Via Calculator Skills." (Illinois State University) *Math Lab Matrix* 5, Spring 1975: 3.

Wehner, Carl. "Pocket Calculators in the Classroom." Iowa Council of Teachers of Mathematics, *I.C.T.M. Journal* 4 (Fall 1975): 22–25.